EXPLORING THE MIDNIGHT WORLD

Christopher Tunney

Designed by David Nash

Illustrators
Mike Atkinson · John Francis

Pan Books · London and Sydney

Each evening, as the sun sets and darkness returns to the world, many wild creatures prepare to sleep. But for other animals the coming of darkness is the signal for them to wake, leave their homes and begin the search for food. These animals are nocturnal, or active at night, and their senses are specially tuned for life in the midnight world.

The Twilight World

As twilight falls over the woods and fields, most of the animals that have been active during the day return to their burrows, nests, or roosts to sleep. Creatures that love the half-light now come into the open to search for food.

Fallow deer browse watchfully on grass, leaves and berries. The badger, leaving its set, is safe from attack. Its body is powerful and its claws sharp. But the timid rabbit has to keep a sharp lookout for badgers, stoats, owls and, above all, the swift and cunning fox.

The polecat, too, is among the rabbit's enemies. It will kill any small mammal it comes across, and will plunge into a stream to seize a frog or an eel. The hedgehog scratches around noisily in the undergrowth, safe beneath its prickly coat. In dark corners, dormice and fieldmice nibble nervously. Above them, the fierce owl sweeps silently through the sky, and the nightjar hunts noisily for moths.

Night Sight

Some night animals that rely mainly on sight to find their way about have huge eyes that let in a great deal of light. When it is dark they can see much more clearly than we can. The owl can spot its prey when there is hardly any light at all. But it is short-sighted and always hunts close to the ground. Most of the animals of the dark can also see well in daylight. Then, the pupils of their eyes become tiny to prevent the lenses being damaged by the strong light.

Night animals do not see in colour. To them, everything in the world is black and white.

day

night

The pupils of an owl's eyes open wide during darkness to let in as much light as possible.

human eye

owl's eye

The owl's eye, with its large lens and tubular shape, has sharper vision than the human eye.

The tarsier leaps from branch to branch at night, hunting for lizards and insects. In relation to its size, it has the largest eyes of all mammals. It lives in south-eastern Asia.

Owls cannot move their eyes at all. To see anywhere but straight ahead they have to move their heads. They are able to turn their heads almost full circle and even upside down. In judging its distance from an object, an owl sometimes bobs its head around, viewing the object from several different angles.

Bats are almost blind but they have no trouble finding their way about. Even in complete darkness they can flit over rooftops, skim through small openings and brush past telephone wires. Hunting for moths, they judge perfectly the zig-zag path of their flight. The bat's skill comes from a special sense of hearing that acts rather like radar. Without it, these flying mammals would be quite helpless.

The pit viper has a sensitive pit or dimple on each side of its head that can detect heat. The warm bodies of the small animals that the pit viper feeds on give out heat. So the snake can find its prey in the dark.

Night-flying moths in search of nectar find flowers mainly by using their keen sense of smell. The flowers' scent is detected by the 'feelers' on the moth's head from some distance away.

A Sixth Sense

Like most animals, we make contact with the world about us by means of our five senses — sight, hearing, taste, smell, and touch or feeling. But some creatures, particularly the animals that are active at night, seem to have a sixth sense. For these animals, the darkness is full of signals that only they can detect.

In most cases, this extra sense is only an increased sharpness of one or more of the five basic senses. But sometimes an animal really has an unusual sense organ. The pit viper, for example, has a heat detector and can sense warm-blooded creatures nearby.

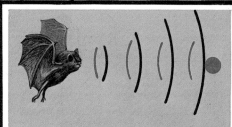

A bat sends out high-pitched sounds which human beings cannot hear. By listening to the echoes of these sounds bouncing back from obstacles in its path, it can fly around safely in the dark.

A fish swimming in the inky darkness of the sea knows that rocks and other obstacles are in its path even before it reaches them. Its sensitive skin feels tiny changes in pressure in the water around the obstacles.

elf owl

coyote

long-tailed
kangaroo rat

Gila monster

sidewinder
snake

scorpion

Night in the Desert

During the day desert animals stay hidden in holes and burrows away from the Sun's burning rays, and the desert looks empty. But at night the desert comes to life, and many different animals appear. The picture shows some of the creatures found in the deserts of North America.

The elf owl flies from its nest hole in a cactus. It scans the ground with its great eyes, searching for the small creatures on which it preys. Among them are rodents, such as mice and the long-tailed kangaroo rat. A gila monster watches a scorpion, while a sidewinder snake looks for prey. The big-eared kit fox prepares to pounce on a lizard. And a coyote skulks around, waiting to pick up what other animals leave behind.

kitfox

banded lizard

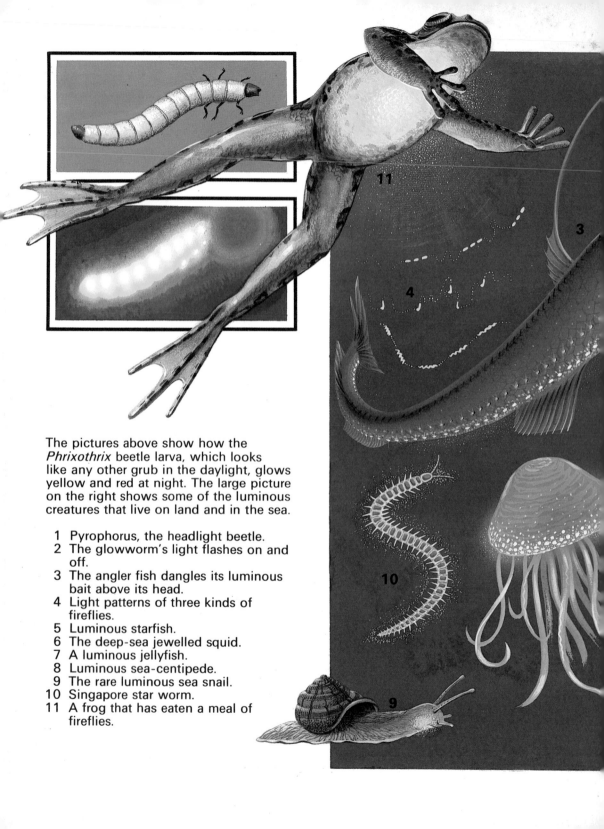

The pictures above show how the
Phrixothrix beetle larva, which looks
like any other grub in the daylight, glows
yellow and red at night. The large picture
on the right shows some of the luminous
creatures that live on land and in the sea.

 1 Pyrophorus, the headlight beetle.
 2 The glowworm's light flashes on and
    off.
 3 The angler fish dangles its luminous
    bait above its head.
 4 Light patterns of three kinds of
    fireflies.
 5 Luminous starfish.
 6 The deep-sea jewelled squid.
 7 A luminous jellyfish.
 8 Luminous sea-centipede.
 9 The rare luminous sea snail.
10 Singapore star worm.
11 A frog that has eaten a meal of
    fireflies.

Living Light

Among the strangest and most beautiful creatures of the dark are those that produce their own light. Some of them are like living luminous jewels. Often, however, they look quite ordinary in daylight. Their light helps them to find their way about at night, to frighten enemies and, sometimes, to attract mates.

Many creatures with their own light are found in the unending darkness of the deep ocean.

Among the best-known creatures with 'living light' are the fireflies that sparkle in bushes and trees on summer evenings. They sometimes lend their light to the frog who eats them. After a meal of fireflies, the frog looks like a small, leaping lantern.

Night in the Jungle

The tropical rain forest is as rich in animal life as it is in plant life. At dusk, many creatures make their way to a river or a jungle pool to drink. Among them is the tiny muntjac or barking deer, whose only defence against attack is flight. The timid creature feels safe in the dark. It does not know that danger is at hand. The tiger which has sheltered from the heat of the day in the cool grass is ready for his evening meal.

The hungry beast watches and waits by the water's edge until the deer bows his head to drink. Then, growling savagely, it springs from its hiding place to kill the helpless creature.

Elephants, too, come down to drink at dusk. But they need not fear attack. They move almost as slowly as the wide-eyed loris which spends the day curled up in a tree. At night, the loris goes for long slow walks among the branches where tree frogs seize their insect prey with long sticky tongues.

If they are not careful, the tree frogs will be seized by another hunter. The python hanging silently and watchfully from a branch is waiting for a chance to strike.

4

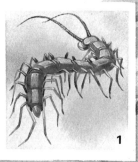

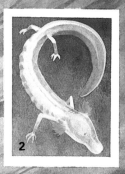

Unending Night

The cave is many worlds in one. For some creatures, including certain salamanders, centipedes and spiders, it is the only world they know. They spend their lives in silence and darkness.

For other creatures, including bats and moths, the cave is a safe home in which to sleep during the hours of daylight. At dusk, there is a flurry of wings as the sleepers waken and take flight into the cool evening air to hunt for food.

Pools of water on the floor of the cave may be the home of animals such as the crayfish. And near the mouth of the cave, many creatures come and go. Among them are earthworms, snails and toads.

1 The centipede hunts for insects in dark, damp places.
2 The blind proteus salamander lives in pools in caves.
3 At night, the crayfish crawls over the bottom of freshwater pools.
4 On damp nights, some earthworms search for leaves which they pull back to their burrows to eat.
5 The snail must keep its body moist. It comes out at night when it is damp.
6 Night-flying moths rest or hide from their enemies during the day.

Francis.

Night in the Garden

At night the garden is quiet. There are no people about to laugh and talk. And the birds that have chirped and twittered in the branches all day are asleep in their roosts. But the moonlit garden is not empty. It only seems deserted because the creatures of the night are quieter than those of the day.

A mole toils steadily through the earth in its search for worms, leaving a tell-tale line of mole-hills across the lawn. A rat sniffs doubtfully at a large stag beetle to see if it would be good to eat. A hedgehog, ambling across a path, has no doubts about the slug it has found. A slug is what it has been looking for all evening.

Near the house, a fox startles itself and everybody else by knocking over a dustbin. It has learnt that there are sometimes tasty titbits inside. A hawkmoth rushes for safety as a bat swoops overhead. And from the garden seat, the domestic cat looks at the busy scene. It is as much a creature of the night as of the day, and is perfectly at home with the other animals of the night.

fairy penguins

Birds of the Night

For many birds, especially those that cannot fly, darkness is a good defence. The small fairy penguin nests in a burrow and comes out at night to catch fish.

The noisy kakapo, a flightless parrot, hides in a burrow until darkness falls. Then it begins its search for food. One of its favourite foods is nectar, and it uses its sense of smell to find flowers in the dark. The kiwi also cannot fly. During the day, it rolls up in a ball to sleep. At night, it scuttles out of its hiding place to scratch about for grubs and worms with its long sharp beak.

kakapos

kiwi

kangaroo

Some of Australia's small marsupial mice leave their nests at night to hunt for insects.

Tasmanian devil

Some of the strangest and rarest animals live in Australia and on the island of Tasmania. The Tasmanian wolf is a fierce doglike creature that stalks the land at night. Few people have ever seen it. The savage Tasmanian devil also hunts at night. It shelters among tree roots or in rocky hollows by day.

The spotted tiger cat lives in Australia. After a night's hunting, it settles down to sleep with its ears folded down to keep out the daytime noises. The timid kangaroos and rock wallabies that live in Australia often come out to graze at night.

For the first six months of its life every kangaroo lives in the dark inside its mother's pouch. Animals that carry their young in pouches are called marsupials. All the animals on this page are marsupials.

ring-tailed rock wallabies

native cat

Tasmanian wolf

Studying the Midnight World

If you are travelling by car along a country road at night, you may catch a glimpse of an animal in the bright headlights. And a quiet walk in the garden after dark with a torch can reveal several night visitors—moths, bats, perhaps an owl or a hedgehog, even a badger if you are very lucky.

But the animals of the midnight world are very shy. Their 'sixth' sense is quick to warn them of danger. To study their habits, you must be quiet and very patient.

Seeing without being Seen

Before he can study nocturnal animals, the naturalist must first know where to find them. He may have to watch all night in a forest clearing or crawl into a damp cave. And it may be many nights before he finds what he is looking for.

To observe the animals properly, he can build a rough shelter or 'hide' from canvas and branches. Inside the hide he can watch without being seen. Provided he approaches upwind (so that the animals do not smell him) and keeps quiet, he is not likely to be noticed.

Recording and Filming

Night binoculars, cameras with special lenses and flash bulbs, and powerful sound recorders are useful aids for the naturalist studying the midnight world.

Badgers have even been shown 'live' on television, leaving their set at night to find food. This was done with the help of infrared cameras, which could film the animals in total darkness.

Night Animals in Zoos

Because they sleep for most of the day, the animals of the midnight world are difficult to see properly in zoos. If they can be seen at all during the day, they are usually sound asleep.

So some zoos have tricked the night animals into thinking that day is night. The animals are housed in a darkened building and their enclosures are lit by special lighting.

Although it is daylight outside, inside it is night. So the animals are wide awake and lively.